Golf Rules O.K.

by
Jim Gregson

To/ Martine,

A little something to amuse you on your flight. I hope you have a great time.

The images in this book made me laugh. and most of them would reflect me playing golf! So be warned if we ever do play a game, you will need to be a good teacher and probably duck a lot.

love Jane
x

A & C Black · London

Published by A & C Black (Publishers) Ltd,
35 Bedford Row, London WC1R 4JH, England

First published 1984
Reprinted 1985, 1988

Gregson, Jim
   Golf rules O.K.
   1. Golf—Rules
   I. Title
   796.352'02'022   GV971
   ISBN 0-7136-2455-8

Cover design and illustrations by William Rudling.
Printed and bound in Great Britain by William Clowes Ltd,
Beccles and London.

Contents

Introduction   5

Your equipment   7
    Clubs   7
    Balls   10

Before you start   12
    Practice   13
    Advice and assistance   15
    Strokes taken   17

On the tee   18
    The 'Honour'   18
    Teeing your ball   18

Through the green   20
    Definition   20
    Plugged balls   21
    Improving your lie or line of play   22
    Striking the ball   24
    Playing the wrong ball   25
    Lifting and dropping   27
    Placing   28
    Identifying your ball   28
    Cleaning your ball   30
    Ball interfering with play   31
    Playing a moving ball   31
    When the ball moves before you play   33
    When another ball strikes yours   34
    Ball unfit for play   34
    Ball lost or out of bounds   36
    Unplayable ball   36
    Provisional ball   39
    Some 'free drops'   40

Hazards   44
    Water hazards   46

The green   48
    The flagstick   48
    On the putting green   50

Other things you should know   56
    The responsibilities of the committee   56
    The responsibilities of the player   57
    Recording scores in stroke play   59
    Playing out of turn   60
    Four-ball and best-ball match play   62

Index   64

Introduction

Golf was conceived as the simplest of all games. It is now governed by the most complex set of rules to enmesh any sport. You may deplore the situation if you like, and be in good company, but if you wish to play this infuriating game you will have to live with it. You cannot even agree with a like-minded opponent to ignore this baroque code, for the formidable catalogue contains this stern admonition:

> Players shall not agree to exclude the operation of any Rule or Local Rule or to waive any penalty incurred.

So you're stuck with the situation, like it or not. Get to know the important rules, and remember that while they may generally seem a formidable hindrance, they can occasionally be a help.

Your equipment

Clubs

The main rule is that you may not carry or use more than fourteen clubs, including your putter. The penalties are severe. If you think them harsh, you might ponder the fact that the fashion for enormous bags and serried ranks of clubs is a quite recent development, no doubt owing much to the now nearly universal presence of the caddie-cart or trolley. Many former giants, including such legends as Harry Varden and J.H. Taylor, managed perfectly well with no more than seven or eight clubs in normal play. Severiano Ballesteros produced the most impressive mastery of shot-making in the modern game by improvising all kinds of shots with two or three clubs as a boy in Spain behind the caddies' hut. If you want more immediate negative evidence, you may watch less gifted figures performing horrifically with fourteen gleaming clubs on almost any course in the world.

If you start a round with fewer than fourteen clubs, you may add as many as will bring you to that number, provided it does not involve unduly delaying play. This might be difficult, since you must not borrow these clubs from any other person playing on the course. Many people think it permissable to borrow a partner's club in a four-ball if they are carrying less than the regulation fourteen maximum. This is not in fact so: they may do so only if the *side* does not carry more than fourteen clubs altogether.

You may replace a club which is damaged in the normal course of play. This, in effect, means while executing a shot; it does not cover the demolition of a club by wrapping it round a tree in the red mist of fury which follows an atrocious shot. I once marked the card of a fine player who had to putt sheepishly with a three-iron for fifteen holes after breaking the shaft of his putter over his knee on failing to hole a two-footer on the third.

You are more likely to break the fourteen-club rule in error than in any attempt to gain advantage, but the severe penalties should warn you against carelessness. In match play you lose a hole for each hole at which the offence occurred, subject to a maximum of two holes in a round. In stroke play, the penalty is two strokes for each hole at which the rule was violated, up to a maximum of four strokes. In Stableford competitions, the penalty is two points per hole, with a maximum of four points per round.

You are not permitted to change the playing characteristics of a club during a round. In 1982, a leading British professional was reported by a fellow competitor and disqualified for doing no more than attaching a piece of sticking plaster to his putter to eliminate the reflection of the sun from the top of the club as he addressed his ball. Such an adjustment would have been perfectly legitimate had he made it before his round commenced. A savage penalty for a tiny technical offence, you may think, but the purpose of this book is to draw attention to the rules and their operation.

. . . you are not permitted to change the playing characteristics of a club . . .

Balls

Weights, sizes and velocities of balls are governed by the Royal and Ancient. You might think that in practice you are no more likely to come across illegal balls than illegal clubs. However, in 1983, an unfortunate girl was disqualified from a major match play championship for using a 'reject' ball, i.e. one with crosses denoting that it did not comply with the maker's normal standards for that ball. All of us who do not have a free supply of balls have played with rejects, often I suspect in competition. Now we know that we should not perpetrate such heinous deceptions!

In the U.K., you may still choose in most club competitions between the small (1.62 in) and the large (1.68 in) ball. The R. and A. is moving gradually towards the universal adoption of the larger ball and many counties already specify the use of the larger ball for their more important competitions. In a few years, uniformity will no doubt prevail and the big ball will be the only one in use. In the meantime, if you plan to use the small ball you should check that it is permitted by the rules of the particular competition: a mistake could mean disqualification. The bigger ball is legal everywhere.

Before you start

Golf courses are divided into four areas, each of which has some rules applicable specifically to it. They are:
(a) The *teeing ground*. The tee-markers will define the forward limits of this: you may play up to two club-lengths behind the line.
(b) *Through the green*. This is the whole area of the course except
   (i) the teeing ground and putting green of the hole being played, and
   (ii) all hazards on the course.
(c) *Hazards*. These are bunkers, water hazards and lateral water hazards.
(d) The *putting green*. Your ball is deemed to be on the putting green when any part of it touches the green.

Some general points of which you should be aware
It will help you if you keep in mind the general penalty for breaches of rules or local rules, which is loss of the hole in match play or two strokes in stroke play. You may take it that these are the penalties for the breaches of rules outlined in the rest of this little book, except where I specify otherwise.

Practice

Most people know the rule that you may not practise on the course on the day of a stroke competition or play-off (although in the case of match-play competitions you may do so unless the Committee decrees otherwise). Less common is the knowledge that you may not practise strokes during the play of any hole, i.e. the common habit of following a horrific stroke by dropping a second ball and trying to produce a better stroke is against the rules.

What *is* allowed? A practice putt on the green of a hole just completed is permissible, except perhaps in the case of a 36-hole stroke-play competition where you are to putt to the same holes in the afternoon round. A practice swing is not a practice stroke and may be taken anywhere on the course provided that no rule is violated.

The 1984 rules revision limited practice to putts or chips on or near the putting green of the hole last played and the next teeing ground. You must not practise from any hazard. Do be aware, with both practice swings and practice putts, of people waiting to play behind you, however, and avoid apoplexy amidst the following group.

. . . be aware of people waiting to play behind you . . .

Advice and assistance

Under the pressure induced by a close game, you may be tempted to ask for more assistance than the rules permit. You may not ask for advice from, or offer advice to, anyone except your partner in a match or either of your caddies. The 1984 revision allowing a team captain or coach to advise his team is unlikely to affect many of us. The most common breach of this rule is in club selection. No one can prevent you from using your eyes or allowing other people to use theirs, but the Machiavellis of golf thrive on the subtleties of misinformation here. Consult any older member of your club for a welter of local folklore on this rule. You will hear tales of 5-wood covers slipped on to 2-woods, of clarion-calls to caddies for 5-irons which by prior arrangement produce 8-irons from those stone-faced accomplices.

More straightforward forms of help are less fraught with malicious human invention. Except on the putting green, anyone may indicate the line of play to you, although they must remove themselves or any marker they have introduced before you play the stroke. Such aid is permitted because it is classed as 'information' about the course rather than 'advice'.

You may cower under your umbrella while you study your ball, but you must have no physical assistance or protection from the elements when actually executing a stroke. On the putting green, your partner or caddie may indicate the line of your putt, but he should not touch the green.

Strokes taken

It is your responsibility to give correct information on this. When you incur a penalty, you should inform your opponent in match play or your marker in stroke play as quickly as possible.

If you are in doubt of your rights or how to proceed, you may play a second ball without penalty, having announced what you are doing to your marker, and telling him which ball you are scoring with if the rules permit it. You must report all the facts to the Committee as soon as you complete your round.

The privilege of playing a second ball in this way does not exist in match play.

On the tee

The 'Honour'

This is simple enough: in a competition you follow the order of the draw on the first tee and thereafter the player, or side, winning a hole retains the honour until a hole is lost. Thankfully, there are no variations here between match and stroke play.

But do you know the procedures in case of violation? In stroke play when a player plays out of turn by mistake the stroke stands, and there is no penalty. In match play, however, his opponent has the option of making him play another stroke in correct order, without penalty.

If you need to play a second ball from the tee, provisional or otherwise, you should do so after the other players have played their first strokes. If you play this second ball out of turn, the provisions outlined above will apply.

Teeing your ball

You may play anything up to two club lengths behind the line of the appropriate tee. Beware of inadvertently playing from outside this rectangle (usually by selecting the wrong tee markers or playing from the wrong side of them). In match play, your opponent may require you to play the stroke from the appropriate place, without penalty. In stroke play, you replay the stroke and are penalised two strokes. If you do not rectify your mistake before you strike from the next tee, or leave the last green if you make the mistake on the last hole, you will be disqualified.

You may stand where you like to address your ball, providing that your ball is within the teeing ground, and if you knock your ball off your tee-peg in addressing it you may re-tee it without penalty. You may also enjoy the luxury of knocking down irregularities in the surface of the tee, an indulgence accorded to you nowhere else on the course. The rules allow you to create or eliminate surface irregularities on the tee; if you wish to avail yourself of such therapy make sure your head greenkeeper or course manager is not of a nervous disposition.

Through the green

Definition

Let us assume that you have negotiated the marshland of preliminary rules and got yourself off the tee. Don't relax! You have merely moved from that dangerous swamp to the firm ground of a minefield. For a start, universally used terms such as 'fairway' don't occur anywhere in the rules of golf. Instead, you have the imprecision of 'closely mown areas' and the mysteries of 'through the green'. You might as well learn to live with this last strange phrase: 'through the green' is the whole area of the course except the teeing ground, the putting green and hazards. The first of these we have already dealt with, the other two we shall arrive at in due course. But first we must confront some of the many delights of the main area of the golf course.

Plugged balls

A ball embedded in its own pitch-mark in a closely mown area (generally 'fairway' to most of us, but including some areas around the greens of par three holes, where there are no fairways) may be lifted and dropped without penalty, as near as possible to the spot where it lay but, as always, not nearer the hole. You may, of course, lift a plugged ball in the rough (you will indeed be well advised to do so to avoid the risk of a hernia, whether physical or psychological) but you are then declaring the ball unplayable and accepting one penalty stroke.

Improving your lie or line of play

The general rule is that you may remove anything not attached to the ground, i.e. stones, twigs, leaves, etc. (loose impediments) but in doing so you must make sure that you do not cause your ball to move.

You must not bend or break anything fixed or growing, or remove or press down sand, loose soil, turf, etc. The important exceptions are adjustments of this sort deriving from (i) your taking your stance and (ii) your execution of the stroke. If you watch any professional tournament, you will see the ingenuity with which seasoned campaigners can 'take a stance'. The change from free-striding young Apollos to arthritic Quasimodos once a ball is located beneath a tree is one of the more beguiling transformations of the professional circuit. Sometimes even a third leg would clearly be welcomed. Here as always you should learn from your golfing betters, deciding the possibilities of 'taking your stance' before thrusting your trunk into whatever simian posture is required to allow your club-head freest access to the ball.

In the rough, you may move long grass, heather, etc. only enough to find and identify your ball. The rules, with that strain of sadism which is never far beneath their surface, remind you that players are not of necessity entitled to see the ball when playing a stroke!

Striking the ball

There are occasions when this will not be straightforward, some of which have just been suggested. You must not push, scrape or spoon the ball (which for ordinary mortals indicates that you must have some degree of backswing). If you strike the ball twice in making a stroke, you count the stroke and add a penalty stroke, making two in all.

Order of striking

The ball furthest from the green should be played first. If you play out of turn in any form of match play, an opponent has the option of requiring you to repeat the shot, without further penalty. In stroke play there is no penalty.

Playing a wrong ball

You must hole out with the ball you played from the teeing ground, except where a rule or local rule permits you to substitute another ball. Inevitably, you will at some time play a wrong ball by mistake.

The penalties are the usual ones: loss of the hole in match play and two-stroke penalty in stroke play. If you are the innocent party and someone has mistakenly played your ball, you place a ball on the spot from which it was played. If you and your opponent inadvertently exchange balls during the play of a hole, the person who first played the wrong ball loses the hole. If this cannot be determined without resort to fisticuffs, you play out the hole with the balls exchanged. It's enough to make you sign the pledge or take to drink, according to your temperament and state of sobriety at the time.

To add piquancy to this appealing rule, there is no penalty for playing the wrong ball in a hazard, provided that you then play the correct ball. I once saw a pork butcher (the occupation may seem irrelevant but to me it had discernible reflections in his bunker play) aim four increasingly savage strokes at a ball embedded in a bunker. The change in his face and language from diabolic fury to angelic serenity as the realisation dawned that the shots

had been played at my ball rather than his own was one of
the most remarkable transformations I have seen in a
game noted for its exploration of the emotional extremes.

The business of playing the wrong ball is especially costly in stroke play. You need to recognise and rectify your mistake before you play from the next tee, or leave the putting green if the error has occurred on the last hole. Even if you have actually holed out before you recognise your error, you may return and play from the correct place, incurring only the two-stroke penalty for playing a wrong ball; the strokes you have played with the wrong ball do not count against you. If, however, you have played from the next tee, or left the putting green in the case of the last hole, you are disqualified from the competition.

Lifting and dropping

Once you have decided to lift a ball under the rules or local rules, anyone you authorise may lift it for you. However, you must drop it yourself. You may have seen fellow members of your club lurching like drunken grizzlies as they prepare for a drop. This diversion is now denied to you by the 1984 rules revision. All you now have to do is stand erect, hold the ball at shoulder height and drop it. You may now face in any direction, instead of towards the hole as formerly. If the ball strikes you or your equipment before or after it hits the ground, you must re-drop, without penalty.

You should drop your ball as near as possible to the spot where it lay, but not nearer the hole, except when a rule permits it to be dropped elsewhere or placed. If your dropped ball rolls into a hazard, out of bounds, on to a putting green, more than two club-lengths from the spot where it landed, or nearer the hole than its original position, you may re-drop without penalty. If the ball rolls into such a position for a second time, you place it where it first struck the ground when re-dropped.

If all that sounds complicated, that is merely because it is! As usual, the complexity arises from having to encompass all eventualities in the rules: if you remember the common sense principle that you should be neither advantaged nor seriously disadvantaged by the behaviour of your ball when you drop it, you will find it a useful guide.

Placing

If, when you place a ball, it fails to remain on the spot where it was placed, you replace it without penalty. If it still proves to have a will of its own, you place it at the nearest spot (not nearer the hole) where it will remain at rest. If you find yourself in such a situation, e.g. on a steep slope in a high wind, you might well study the ball carefully before you address it, examining it carefully for any sign of whimsical intentions. For remember that if it moves after you have addressed it, there will be a penalty stroke, as well as unfeeling hilarity among insensitive onlookers.

Remember that once you have dropped or placed your ball correctly, it is in play and must not be re-dropped or re-placed except as provided in the rules.

Identifying your ball

You should put an identification mark on your ball in addition to the maker's normal markings. As the responsibility for playing the correct ball is entirely yours, you may lift it to identify it, except in a hazard. You must replace it exactly on the spot from where it was lifted, in the presence of your opponent (match play) or marker (stroke play) and you must not clean it, beyond what is necessary for identification. If you lift a ball to identify it in a hazard, you will be penalised one stroke.

. . . if it moves after you have addressed it . . .

Cleaning your ball

Generally, you will have to wait until you arrive at the
putting green to clean your ball. You may clean it,
however, whenever you lift under penalty (unplayable lies,
water hazards, etc.) or without penalty (casual water,
ground under repair, plugged ball, etc.) or when a local
rule permits it (winter rules are the commonest instance:
they are local rules and you will need to study their
particular wording about placing, cleaning and distances).

If you lift or clean your ball when the rules do not
permit it, there is a penalty of one stroke.

Ball interfering with play

Through the green or in a hazard, you may have any ball lifted which you consider interferes with your play. The ball should be marked in the normal manner and replaced after your stroke.

Playing a moving ball

You may not play while your ball is moving. It is difficult to imagine, even in a game notable for a lengthy catalogue of eccentricities, those who would wish to do so deliberately. There are, however, occasions when you might hit a moving ball through forces beyond your control. The rules do not admit a haze of thunderous anger as one of these, so that the fourth successive savage slash at a ball re-descending the face of a bunker incurs a penalty. But if a stroke is made at a ball which falls off a tee-peg, there is no penalty, although the stroke counts. Similarly, if a ball moves after you have begun your backswing, there is no penalty for hitting it while it is moving, although again the stroke counts.

Those with a taste for the bizarre should note that it is permitted to make a stroke at a moving ball in a water hazard, without penalty. On one memorable occasion I used the provision to aim a savage 5-iron at a ball nosing its way gently downstream and being studied with malicious glee by my opponent, Derek Fowles, a retired bank manager from whom such misanthropic conduct might be expected. It was one of the few totally satisfactory strokes to be executed in such a situation: the ball only marginally cleared the further edge of the water hazard, but the malign Fowles was drenched in an evil green spray which was most uplifting to the spirits of three members of our four-ball.

When the ball moves before you play

If any outside agency moves your ball, you simply replace it and play on without penalty, though you should note that the rules state whimsically that neither wind nor water is an outside agency!

Be careful when searching for your ball. You may think you have suffered enough in arriving in the rough, but if you, your partner, your equipment or either of your caddies moves the ball accidentally in searching, there is a penalty stroke. Should anyone else move it, you can replace it and play on without penalty.

You may move loose impediments as outlined above (see 'Improving your lie'), but if your ball moves after you have removed any loose impediments within a club-length, you incur a penalty stroke.

If you think your ball may be about to move as you prepare to address it, you would do well to wait for a moment, for if the ball moves after you have addressed it, the rules decree a penalty stroke. The commonest example of this is on the green when you replace your ball after cleaning it, particularly if there is a high wind: twice my ball has moved as I prepared to putt, to the accompaniment on each occasion of a manic yell of delight from Derek Fowles, who has an unhappy knack of being present at such times.

One bright spot in this dark world: if you touch your ball with your club in addressing it, there is no penalty, provided that it does not move. For this purpose 'move' means to leave its position and come to rest elsewhere, i.e. if your ball settles back into its original position, there is no penalty.

When another ball strikes yours

The 1984 rules revision introduced consistency here. In all forms of play, if a ball at rest is moved by another ball, the moved ball must be replaced and the other ball played as it lies.

Ball unfit for play

You may replace your ball without penalty if it is so damaged that its flight or roll will be affected. You may not change it merely because mud adheres to it, or its surface is scratched or discoloured. Before substitution you should obtain the agreement of your opponent, or marker, that your ball is unfit for play. You may lift your ball to check its condition after you have announced your intentions to him. If a ball breaks into pieces as a result of a stroke (many of the newer types of ball are of solid rather than traditional construction and will eventually crack or disintegrate completely, though they are in other respects more durable than rubber-cored balls), you may place a ball where the original one lay and play again, without penalty.

Ball lost or out of bounds

In effect, a bad stroke of this kind costs you two strokes (except where you lose your ball in a water hazard), since the rule is that you play again from the same spot and add a penalty stroke (usually referred to as 'stroke and distance'). On the tee, you tee again wherever you like; through the green or in a hazard you drop the ball as near as possible to the same spot. In playing, the important point is always the position of your ball, not yourself — you may stand out of bounds to play if you so wish.

Unplayable ball

For once you are the sole judge of this. You may declare your ball unplayable anywhere on the course except in a water hazard. Having done so you either:

(a)   proceed as above under 'lost ball' (i.e. go back and repeat the stroke, with the same penalties — in effect, two strokes); or

(b)   drop a ball within two club-lengths of where the ball lay, not nearer the hole, under penalty of one stroke; or

(c)   drop a ball behind the point where the ball lay, keeping that point between yourself and the hole; you may go back as far as you like on this line, under penalty of one stroke.

As common sense would indicate, if you declare your ball unplayable in a bunker, the ball must be dropped in the bunker if you are proceeding under (b) or (c).

What this means for practical purposes is that you will find in almost all cases that you can declare your ball unplayable for one penalty stroke and give yourself a reasonable shot, either within two club-lengths or much further back on the line indicated. On rare occasions (e.g. deep in woods or in intractable heather, when you wonder why on earth you gave up cricket) you may have nowhere suitable to drop and be forced to accept the greater penalty of replaying the original shot.

Do be prepared to use this rule and accept the one-stroke penalty normally involved. On any British golf course on any Sunday morning you can see high handicappers, as prodigal with strokes as with our noble language, profaning the Sabbath as they hack savagely at balls which professionals would not tackle.

Provisional ball

If you think your ball may be lost or out of bounds, you may play a provisional ball to save time. The important thing to remember is that you should declare whether it is a provisional ball or the 'ball in play' (i.e. that you have deemed your previous ball lost) *before* you play it. If you fail to declare the ball as a provisional it becomes the ball in play, under penalty of stroke and distance, and the original ball is deemed to be lost.

You may continue to play strokes with the provisional ball until you reach the spot where the original ball is likely to be, but if you play a stroke nearer to the hole than this spot, the original ball is deemed lost.

If the original ball is lost (except in a water hazard) or out of bounds, the provisional becomes your ball in play with two strokes penalty (stroke and distance). If the original ball is found in play, the provisional ball must be abandoned, however horrific the position of the original. You must search for no longer than five minutes.

Some 'free drops'

(i) *Obstructions*: 'obstructions' are artificial objects erected, placed or left on the course. Movable obstructions may be removed without penalty if they impede you: beware of hernias and coronaries incurred in proving objects are movable.

You may also have relief from immovable obstructions without penalty if the ball lies in, on, or so close to them as to interfere with your stance or swing; the mere fact that an object is on your line of play is not enough to warrant relief. You drop within one club-length of the nearest point of relief which is not nearer the hole, and not in a hazard or on a putting green. There is no relief from immovable obstructions in water hazards.

(ii) *Casual water*: this is any temporary accumulation of water visible before or after you have taken your stance. If the ball lies in the water or it affects your stance or swing, you may drop as above. In a hazard you drop as near as possible to where the ball lay on the gound which affords you maximum relief from the water, but this must be within the hazard.

On the green you may claim relief if water lies between you and the hole. You place the ball in the nearest position which affords maximum relief and is not nearer the hole or in a hazard, i.e. not any position on the green which suits you.

(iii) *Ground under repair* is any portion of the course so marked, and you may drop from it without penalty as above.

(iv) *Holes made by burrowing animals* stretch the imaginations of some golfers. Birds and snakes are included as animals. I once saw strong men almost come to blows over whether a worm constituted a 'burrowing animal', such is the charm of this ancient game and of the British character under stress. I forbore to suggest that worm casts were covered by the rule allowing the removal of loose impediments lest I should impede the development of moral fibre in the participants in this interesting debate.

When a ball is lost in casual water, ground under repair or a hole made by a burrowing animal, you may drop another one without penalty within a club length of the point where the ball crossed the margin of the area, not nearer the hole. In a hazard you must, as usual, drop the new ball in the hazard to avoid penalty. There is no relief from holes made by burrowing animals or immovable obstructions in water hazards.

The rules state that there must be reasonable evidence that a ball has been lost in this way. In practice, this means that your opponent or marker must agree that the ball was lost in one of these three situations and not on the rest of the course. Although the unchivalrous Fowles has been known to become suddenly myopic under stress, there is generally little problem with normal beings.

If a ball is not immediately visible in casual water, ground under repair or a hole made by a burrowing animal, the rules allow you to probe for it. You may find yourself a source of interest to passing non-golfers on some courses when doing this; you should remember Chesterton's admonition to the fat man chasing his hat and think not of your own discomfiture and embarrassment but of the innocent amusement you are providing for others.

You may also play from these situations if you prefer this to relief without penalty: occasionally it may pay you to do this, particularly from ground under repair.

Hazards

The initial point to remember in hazards is that you must not ground your club in addressing the ball. You may place your feet firmly in taking your stance, but not otherwise test the surface of a hazard. Most people know that they should not touch the sand with the club in a bunker until the shot is played, but many forget that the rule applies to all hazards. Thus, although it is quite permissible to play from within the margins of a water hazard (and don't forget that these may sometimes be quite dry, with an illogicality peculiar to the rules of golf), you should not ground your club there, nor touch water with your club before playing your shot.

Some clubs have a local rule permitting the removal of stones from bunkers before playing, but you should check the card before doing so: this is not a rule of golf. If the ball is covered by sand, fallen leaves, etc., you may remove as much of this material as will enable you to see the top of the ball. If you move your ball in such a search, there is no penalty; the ball must be replaced, unless you opt for a drop under penalty. Remember that you may not lift your ball for identification in a hazard, but that no penalty is incurred for playing the wrong ball there (see p. 26).

Shots played from water have delights which are peculiarly their own, some of which I touched upon earlier. Generally it is advisable to ensure that they are played by your opponent rather than yourself and that you stand well clear.

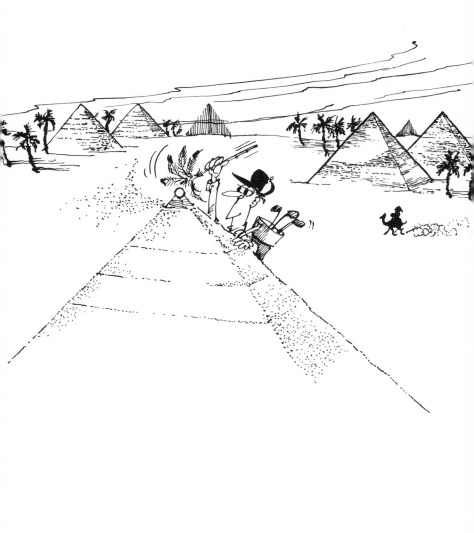

Water hazards

Remember that if you lose a ball in a water hazard the penalty is only one shot, the same as if you find it and choose to drop. You drop behind the water hazard, keeping the point at which your ball crossed its margin between you and the hole and going back as far as you like. You may also drop for the same one-stroke penalty as near as possible to where the original stroke was played, but clearly you will only wish to do this in exceptional circumstances.

Lateral water hazards

By definition these are water hazards from which it is impracticable or impossible to drop a ball behind the water while keeping the spot where you entered it between you and the hole. If you decide to drop, you do so within two club-lengths of *either* the point at which your ball last crossed the margin of the hazard *or* a point on the opposite margin of the hazard equidistant from the hole.

The green

If you have survived this Pilgrim's Progress of
Disillusionment so far, take courage — the end is in sight!
Only the green, with its labyrinthine subtleties of contour
and rules, remains to be negotiated.

The flagstick

You may have the flagstick attended at any time, whether
you are on the green or off it. On one notable occasion,
Walter Hagen sent his caddie forward well over a hundred
yards to attend, but such flamboyant optimism is not
recommended to ordinary mortals. You must decide
whether you want the flagstick left, attended or removed; if
it is attended or removed without explicit direction but with
your knowledge you will be deemed to have authorised it
if you raise no objection.

   You may, of course, strike the unattended flagstick
when playing from anywhere off the green, but that is all.
On all other occasions, you will suffer the penalty of two
strokes in stroke play and loss of hole in match play. These
occasions include your ball striking the flagstick when it is
attended or removed (e.g. when it is lying on the ground
some distance from the hole) and when it is unattended
but you have putted from on the green. The penalty is the
same when you strike a person rather than the flagstick, or
equipment of someone attending the flagstick with your
knowledge or authority.

   When your ball comes to rest against the flagstick,
you or the person you authorise should remove the
flagstick carefully so that your ball drops into the hole. If it
goes anywhere else, you have to putt it from the edge of
the hole.

On the putting green

You may repair ball pitch marks and move sand, soil and loose impediments by picking them up or brushing them aside with your hand or club. If you move your ball, it may be replaced without penalty. You are not allowed to press anything down: you may have seen professionals tapping down stud marks, but they will have had special P.G.A. dispensations to do so, not accorded to ordinary fallible players like us.

You may lift and clean your ball anywhere on the putting green, marking it with a ball-marker or coin before you do so. If your marker then interferes with another player's stroke it should be moved one or more putterhead-lengths to one side.

Your partner or caddie may help you with the line of a putt, but the line of the putt must not be touched, even behind the hole. No mark should be placed on the green to indicate a line for putting, though of course no one can prevent you from using anything already there. You should not 'test the surface of the putting green by rolling a ball' during the play of a hole. If you have an opponent with the approach of Derek Fowles, he may claim you are doing this when you generously concede a putt and knock his ball back to him.

Strictly speaking, you should lift it or leave him to do so. (But it is worth noting, should you associate or be drawn in competition with persons of such dubious ethical stature, that the rules state that when you concede a putt you can remove your opponent's ball with a club or otherwise. Machiavelli would have loved golf.)

If your ball comes to rest overhanging the edge of the hole, you are allowed a few seconds to see if it drops into the hole, but no elephantine leaps to assist it to do so. Usually you will have to decide it has come to rest and accept the ultimate golfing paradox, the half-inch tap-in that counts the same on your card as the 250-yard drive.

In connection with this, you should note that standing astride or on the line of your putt is prohibited, a rule introduced some years ago to outlaw 'croquet-type' putting. You may think, as I do, that anything which makes putting easier and thus diminishes its importance within the overall game is to be applauded: alas, the rules do not support us and we must suffer in silence.

If your ball comes to rest on a putting green other than that of the hole you are playing, you drop clear of the green without penalty. You find the point nearest to where your ball lies which is also no nearer to the hole and not in a hazard; you then drop within one club-length of this spot.

. . . no penalties in match play for a ball striking another ball . . .

Many players are unclear about their rights to have an opponent's ball left or removed on the green. The 1984 revision simplified and standardised the procedure. You may at any time, in any form of golf, have a ball lifted if you consider that it interferes with your play. Similarly, you may lift your ball if you consider that it might assist your opponent. In other words, the rule which has applied for many years to three- and four-ball match play now extends to all forms of match play. If a ball at rest is moved by another ball, it must be replaced and the other ball played as it lies. There are no penalties in any type of match play for a ball hitting another ball. In stroke play, if, when both balls are on the putting green, your putt strikes a fellow competitor's ball, there is a penalty of two strokes.

Other things you should know

The responsibilities of the committee

Apart from being the unofficial scapegoat for all the club's ills, the committee has official duties assigned to it by golf's governing body. The committee or its authorised representative should define accurately:

(i) The course and its bounds (white stakes).
(ii) The margins of water hazards (yellow stakes) and lateral water hazards (red stakes).
(iii) Ground under repair.
(iv) Obstructions.

The committee should ensure that new holes are cut on the day on which a stroke competition commences and at such other times as it considers necessary. It is the committee, or its authorised representative, which decides when the course is unplayable and suspends or cancels play.

The most important role of most committees is as maker and publisher of local rules. The committee has no power to waive a rule of golf or the penalty imposed by a rule of golf.

The responsibilities of the player

You are responsible for acquainting yourself with the conditions of any competition in which you take part. You are allowed one caddie, but only one, the penalty for any breach being disqualification. (Those golfers with enthusiastic supporters within the family, a benefit which has never embarrassed the writer, should beware of unwitting transgression of this rule.)

. . . you are allowed one caddie, but only one . . .

The new system of handicapping has recently led to confusions. It is your responsibility to play to your current official handicap. The new system of handicapping is based on purely arithmetical adjustments, but the old ruling that no one may adjust his own handicap *upwards* prevails.

You must wait for a new, higher handicap to be posted officially within the clubhouse before adopting it. On the other hand, when you have played a round which means a *downward* adjustment in your handicap, you must immediately adopt this lower handicap in stroke and match play. If you play off a higher handicap than you should, you will be disqualified from any handicap competition; if you play off a lower one, your score, or the result of your match, will stand.

In match play, you may discontinue play by mutual agreement, providing the competition is not delayed. Otherwise, you may discontinue play only if you consider there is danger from lightning or there is some emergency, such as sudden illness, which the committee accepts as satisfactory.

You must play at all times without undue delay. The interpretation of this phrase is so subjective that it is almost impossible for the rule to be applied: hence the deplorable proliferation of slow play in professional and (unpardonably) in club competitions. Only severe arthritis would excuse the progress of some young and fit members of every club through the green; on the green cerebral paralysis appears to take over as they consider a putt. Slow play is breaking the rules: one can only applaud those few clubs and associations which attempt to enforce the rules in this difficult area.

Recording scores in stroke play

You are responsible for recording the scores of the competitor whose card you have been given to mark in a competition, and checking with him after each hole that the figure you are recording is the correct one. On

. . . deplorable proliferation of slow play . . .

completion of the round, you sign the card and hand it to the competitor. On receipt of your own score-card, you are solely responsible for checking the scores for each hole and ensuring that your marker has signed the card. You should settle any doubtful points with the committee and return your card as soon as possible.

After your card has been returned to the committee, no alteration may be made to it. A score for any hole lower than that actually taken will mean disqualification; a score higher than that actually taken must stand as returned.

Playing out of turn

If an opponent plays when you should have done, you may make him replay in correct order, without penalty, providing you do so immediately.

In three-ball match play, each player is playing two distinct matches. You need to remember this principle if you are not to be carried off by men in white coats amidst the simulated sympathy of your two opponents. For instance, if your ball strikes that of one of your opponents, his equipment or his caddie, you have two different match situations to consider. In that against the offender, you may play the ball as it lies or replay the stroke from the original spot. In your match against the other opponent, you must treat the occurrence as a rub of the green and play out the hole with your original ball.

. . . two distinct matches . . .

I once saw an unfortunate playing with Derek Fowles and myself in a three-ball who was beset with a bout of shanking on the fifteenth. He hit first my trolley and then that of the formidable Fowles, who was already deep in his rule book at the time. This normally sturdy fellow was forced by the delighted Fowles to play out the hole with three different balls (please work this out for yourself) to the consternation of the match behind us who accused him of holding up the course by practising. This fourteen-stone golfer of steady nerve left the course a broken man and gave up the game for several months.

Four-ball and best-ball match play

Throughout the hole, balls belonging to the same side may be played in the order the side prefers.

If your ball strikes yourself, your partner or either of your caddies or equipment, you are disqualified from the hole, but your partner incurs no penalty.

If it strikes an opponent or his caddie or equipment there is no penalty; you have the option of playing the ball as it lies or replaying the stroke immediately from the same spot. If you play a wrong ball, you are disqualified from the hole but your partner is not affected. If you accidentally move your partner's ball, he, not you, incurs the penalty stroke. This is a test of friendship I do not recommend you to undertake.

If one member of a side carries more than fourteen clubs, the side is penalised. One of the highlights of my

golfing career, which seems to have had more than the normal quota of triumphs and disasters, was the discovery that Derek Fowles's partner was carrying two putters and thus one club too many on the seventeenth. Fowles was about to win two and one, and although he had only seven clubs in a carrying bag, suffered the penalties of his partner's transgression and lost the match. So often a delighted invoker of the sacred rules himself, he accepted his fate on this occasion with as much grace as he could muster — that is to say, none at all.

At last, an easy shot . . .

Index

advice, 15–16
attending flagstick, 48

ball
    hitting flagstick, 48
    interfering with play, 31
    lost, 36
    moving after address,
        33–4
    moved by another, 34
    moved by outside agency,
        33
    moved during search, 33
    sizes, 10
    striking player or
        equipment, 62–3
    unfit for play, 34
bunkers, 44

caddies, 15–16, 56, 62
checking scores, 59–60
cleaning ball, 30
club modifications, 9
clubs
    numbers of, 7, 62–3
    replacing, 8
committee, duties of, 56

dropping a ball, 27–8

green, 48–55

handicaps, 57–8
hazards, 44–7
hitting ball twice, 24

identifying ball, 28, 44

lateral water hazards, 47
lifting ball, 27, 55
loose impediments, 22

marking a ball on
    green, 51

order of striking, 18, 25,
    60–1
out of bounds, 36

placing a ball, 28
playing a moving
    ball, 31–2
playing wrong
    ball, 25–7
plugged balls, 21
practice, 13
provisional ball, 39
putting stances, 52

repairing pitch marks, 50

scores, recording of, 58
slow play, 58
stones in bunkers, 44

teeing the ball, 18–19

unplayable ball, 36–8

water hazards, 46